CAKEWALK

The Science of Happy

* LAW OF ATTRACTION FOR TEENS & TWEENS *

CJ STAPLES & LILY NESS

Hi Joy!
Thank you for supporting our project!
Wishing you much ease, joy, & Love, CJ

The Science of Happy

* LAW OF ATTRACTION FOR TEENS & TWEENS *

BY CJ STAPLES & LILY NESS

Think-Ink Publishing, Minneapolis

Copyright © 2018 by Cj Staples; Illustrations copyright 2017 by Cj Staples

All rights reserved. No portion of this book may be reproduced—mechanically, electronically, or by any other means, including photocopying—without written permission of the author. Reviewers may quote brief passages in reviews.

DISCLAIMER
Neither the author nor the publisher assumes any responsibility for errors, omissions, or contrary interpretations of the subject matter herein. Any perceived slight of any individual or organization is purely unintentional. Brand and product names are trademarks or registered trademarks of their respective owners.

978-1-7320899-0-7
Library of Congress Catalog Number: 2018903901
Published in United States; First Printing: 2018

COVER AND DESIGN BY HEIDI MILLER
HeidiMillerDesignMpls.com

PHOTOGRAPHY BY CJ STAPLES & LILY NESS THINK-INK PUBLISHING
P.O. Box 301, Mound MN 55364
cj@cjstaples.com | cakewalklife.com
Reseller discounts available.

EDITING BY SHARON PAYNE

TABLE OF CONTENTS

1

Intro

4

How to get the most out of this book

    5 You are invited

6

CHAPTER 1 **What is LOA?**

    7 What is LOA?

    9 Energy

    11 Alignment

        12 *Lily: Practice makes perfect*

    13 Attraction

        13 *How do you attract something you want?*

16

CHAPTER 2 **Relationships**

    17 You, Yourself, and You

        17 *Who are you?*

    19 Being Self-ish

        20 *Lily*

        20 *Alone time*

    21 Your Inner-Being

        21 *Role models*

        23 *Be nicer to your-self*

    26 Friends and Foes?

        26 *Fitting in and being confident*

        26 *Lily*

    28 Feeling Like a Victim

        31 *Drama*

        31 *Using empathy vs sympathy in the face of drama*

        32 *Peer pressure*

        34 *Don't be jelly!*

        36 *The three sad stooges: negative, pessimistic, and gloomy*

40 Family Dynamics

    40 *Parents and expectations — What do you want from me?*

    41 *Divorce*

    43 *Sibling rivalry*

46 Teachers, Coaches, Bosses, and Preachers

    47 *Teachers*

    47 *Lily*

    47 *Coaches*

48 Dating

    48 *I'm not that into you — being rejected*

    49 *Pressure and respecting boundaries*

    51 *Lily*

52

CHAPTER 3 **Thoughts and Beliefs**

53 What Are You Thinking?

53 Letting Go of the Little Things

    55 *Lily*

    56 *"Tell me what you want, what you really, really want!"*

    56 *Taking action*

    58 *Your emotions*

59 Stress — School, Homework, and Sports

    59 *Lily's own story*

    62 *Sadness*

    63 *In a funk*

    64 *Listening to your intuition*

    66 *Imagination*

68 Believe It and You Will See It

    68 *What are beliefs?*

69 What If You Don't Get What You Want?

69 What Others Believe

72

CHAPTER 4 **It's Your Life**

73 Why Am I Here?

73 Your Future

73 *Whatcha gonna do*

77 *Seriously*

78 *How do you want to feel?*

79 What is the Story You Are Telling?

79 *It's your story — Tell an epic one!*

79 *Appreciate everything*

81 You Get to Choose

81 *What if I make a mistake in my choosing, or what I want doesn't show up?*

81 *Magical thinking makes you a Master Manifester: What do you choose?*

86
Afterword

88
Remember to Share

90
Giving Back

91
Resources and Recommendations

92
About Cj

93
About Lily

94
Thank You From Cj

95
Thank You From Lily

96
From Us

iNTRO

CAKEWALK — You might be wondering why we chose Cakewalk as the title for this book. It has a varied background and appears to have come about sometime in 19th century as a kind of fancy dance or walk performed by southern African-Americans with a cake being the prize for the best performance. It became a widespread dance fad sometime in the 1890s.

The figurative definition adopted is "something easy." Lily and I found that we love both the word and the definition, as it describes how we all should be in life.... Easy, Cool, Stylish, Fancy, and Joyful, as we do our best "Cakewalk" through life. We encourage you to practice and play with the exercises in this book and in doing so you will have a wonderful and fun life experience, with cake! Enjoy!

FROM CJ

Hey!

I'm Cj. I am a Joyful Living Coach and entrepreneur. My lovely granddaughter Lily, 17, and I are the authors and illustrators of this book. We are happy you are here reading this book. It means you are an awesomely unique individual wanting to live the very best life possible! Congrats!

In writing this book, we hope that you will learn something about Law of Attraction (LOA) or, as we like to call it, "The science of Happy" and can then choose to practice it in your life and come to understand your life in a whole new way. Seriously... life is fun, it doesn't have to be as hard or difficult as we sometimes make it, and you always have a choice in how you feel about any subject, wanted or unwanted. And who doesn't want to feel good and have fun, right??!

Inside this book, you will find stories, quotes, tips, and exercises you can do, if you choose, that will make it easier to understand and practice these teachings.

We hope you find Cakewalk an entertaining and insightful read that leaves you excited to test and practice these laws yourself to find out just how much control you have in your life based on the thoughts and things you choose to focus on. We also hope you simply have fun. Don't overthink it.

FROM LILY

Hey!

I'm Lily. I am 17 years old, I love photography or anything else that involves being creative. I've always been a glass half full kinda person, so when I started studying LOA, it explained a lot. I have been studying *Abraham Hicks Law of Attraction for about four years now. When I was first learning it, it confused me a bit because of the big way they spoke of The Vortex. I had many questions that I would ask my mother and grandma to understand, so they could put it into a way I could understand. It has changed the way I look at things in life: I am easier (most of the time) about the tough things that happen and simply a happier person when I look through my rose-colored glasses. I want this book to be a way for people my age to understand and relate LOA to their real life, so they can apply it to make life and situations lighter.

*Abraham Hicks – Jerry and Esther Hicks are the founders of the Abraham Hicks teachings of Law of Attraction. Esther Hicks connects with Abraham or "infinite intelligence" and shares with anyone wanting to understand and have more fun in life.

HOW TO GET THE MOST OUT OF THIS BOOK

We recommend that you take your time and do the exercises outlined, and that you read and practice a section each night just before going to bed. This will help you fall asleep and wake up feeling refreshed, inspired, excited, and free.

You were born into a wonderful time of human growth and expansion! There is a larger and larger population starting to understand the laws of the Universe and because of that, it is becoming, and will continue to become, the norm. There is so much power in understanding your positive energy. You are on the leading edge of inspired thought.

As you read and learn this material, you will notice and be more aware than ever before of how you are feeling in situations that might have been difficult for you to deal with in the past. Those situations will feel easier, you will respond differently, and have better outcomes than ever before.

The Science of Happy 5

WE INVITE YOU TO WRITE AND SHARE YOUR STORIES!

We will be taking submissions for our next book, and we would love to share your success stories based on what you learn from this little book. How fun is that?! See details on page 88.

Parents, you are also invited to share stories or insights of what you have observed as your teen/tween learns and practices this information.

Now, let's get started on this exciting journey of Ease and Awesomeness!

CHAPTER ONE

What is LOA?

WHAT IS LOA?

Law of Attraction, LOA, is quantum physics. It is not a religion or a belief system that is created or made up. It just is. It is not anti-anything. We like to call it "The science of Happy." LOA is based on energy, and, like a magnet, what we focus or put our energy on is what we attract to us. You can still happily practice your chosen faith and spiritual beliefs and learn LOA at the same time.

> **EVERYTHING IS ENERGY AND THAT'S ALL THERE IS TO IT. MATCH THE FREQUENCY OF THE REALITY YOU WANT, AND YOU CANNOT HELP BUT GET THAT REALITY. IT CAN BE NO OTHER WAY. THIS IS NOT PHILOSOPHY. THIS IS PHYSICS.**
> ALBERT EINSTEIN

Here is an example of what is common thinking in today's world:

> *Luke's dad loves to watch the news during dinner time. As he does, he grunts, groans, and grumbles: "The world is in shambles. You can't trust anybody these days," and things like that. Luke has heard this over and over again, and he too has become angry because he has picked up the energy of all that. He is often wondering why things don't go his way and when he will catch a break. He wonders what is wrong with the world and is fearful about what the future holds for himself and his family. He wishes there was something he could do to make things feel better because it certainly doesn't feel good right now.*

What Luke and his father don't understand is that thoughts become things and what is focused on with great emotion becomes reality.

> One day, Luke walks into town for his guitar lesson. As he passes a gift shop, a sign in the window catches his eye. It says: "What you think, you become." And he stops in his tracks and reads it again. "Whoa," he thinks "Could that really be true? If it is, am I going to grow up frustrated or angry at the world?" He knows his dad wants to be happy and enjoying his life, but he knows that often he is not. "What does it mean? Is it simply not giving so much attention on the negative things that feel so bad? What if I could be informed, but not emotionally invested in things I cannot control?" Hmm... "What have I got to lose?" he thinks as he walks on. "Why not give it a try?"

ENERGY

Einstein, Jesus, Buddha, and thousands of others throughout time, have known and understood that everything is energy or vibration: you in your physical body, your thoughts, the ground you walk on, the sky you look up at, your puppy, your glass, and the water in it. (Check out "The Hidden Messages in Water" — by Masaru Emoto for wonderful images showing how water responds to our energy.) It is like we are holding a great big magnet of energy and we attract what we give our attention to. The thoughts we choose, either positive or negative, will attract more like them to it, and that affects our experience in life. Don't worry, you won't have a terrible experience today because of something you thought last night. Both positive and negative thoughts become things when they are practiced over and over and you then believe what you are thinking.

So, practicing a positive energy/vibration will produce positive results in life. How cool is it to know that? It is like having a superpower that most people are completely unaware of. Once you learn to attract what you desire, you have positive energy that people can feel, even if they don't know why, and they will be wanting to hang out with you and just be in your positive energy field. The ones who are usually more negative won't be hanging with you anymore, and if they do show up, your energy won't dip down, at least not for long, because you have learned alignment, and feeling good is what you've chosen to do most.

Once you start to learn this information, you will start to see all kinds of things happening in your life that will prove to you that you are a powerful creator. Of course, as with anything in life, the choice is all yours to play or not. There really are no rules except to do your best to choose happy as often as possible! And then watch what shows up for you. Here are a few examples of what can happen:

- You find yourself meeting or hanging with really awesome people whom you never thought you would hang out with before.

- You start getting better grades.

- People begin to treat you with more kindness.

- You are given an opportunity for a part-time job that you weren't expecting.

- You find yourself laughing and smiling more.

- You hardly ever feel angry, sad, or frustrated, and when you do, it doesn't last long.

- Things or situations you have wanted start to show up in the most surprising and unexpected ways.

ALiGNMENT

Being in alignment is the term we use when we're referring to being in touch with your inner-being, your soul, your true self, and you're feeling good. Not just the "yeah, I'm fine" kind of good, but the kind of feeling good that you experience and you wish you could feel that way all the time. Like when you were little, and you got to go to a movie or to an ice cream shop and you totally freaked like you won a trip to Disney World!!! Ok, maybe you still do that. We sure do!

We were all born to feel good and have joy. Why then is it that, as people grow up, they seem to experience more and more negative emotion? Well, it is a learned thing. Many teachings in our society, our media, and our culture in general insist that struggle is the way to get what we want in life. Our parents learned it from their parents, who learned it from their parents, and so on. So, while they/

we all mean well, we pass along both our positive emotions as well as our negative ones to our children. Even the most positive, aligned parents and people in the world have "mind-junk" or negative beliefs that don't serve them well. After all, most are still believing that you must struggle to get anywhere in life. Doesn't taking happy and aligned action sound way more fun?!

Learning this material at a young age sets you up for a more joyful life experience because when you are young, you are more connected to your inner-being and you haven't picked up the mind-junk of the world around you.

As with anything you want to learn and do well, it takes practice. When you learn to quiet your mind and use your imagination, your inner-being will respond, saying: yes, I want to do that. And you will become like a magnet, attracting the people, situations, or ideas that bring you to, or closer to, helping you to define your desires. That is when you feel the Magic of it!

You know how you played pretend as a small child and you could really imagine that you were the princess or the astronaut flying to the moon, and it felt very real to you? You were in alignment as you played and imagined it and it felt good to you. Pretending is a great thing. It helps you to see what it is you really desire and allows you to play around with it and experiment until it feels just right to you. The key to alignment is feeling good. It doesn't matter if it is actually here yet, but only that thinking of it feels good.

Lily: Practice makes perfect

Sometimes I get in some slumps, we all do, it's normal! Even for the people who study the science of happy. It's a common misconception that all contrast will go away if you study this, but keep in mind that different situations and emotions are the reason we know what we do want and what we don't want. Learning LOA gives you the right tools to deal with things in an easier way or to help you stop it before it snowballs. Contrast is a part of everyone's life. Things will happen from time to time, but it's all about how you handle it.

For example.... let's say I failed a test and it gets me down. I could think to myself, "Hey you know this kinda stinks, but you know it's one test out of many and my life will go on. I can always talk to my teacher for extra credit or do a retake. All is well." Just take a breath and remind yourself this is not forever. It might take a couple of tries to flip your thinking so start with the little things. Practice turning those negative "I don't want this" thoughts into positive "this is what I learned, and this is what I want" thoughts. Then give yourself a pat on the back because you are the most expanded and smart version of you!

ATTRACTION

How do you attract something you want?

Whether it's a situation or a material object, first you need to know what you want. Sounds easy, right? Yet sometimes we don't know exactly what we want. Or we think we want something only to find that it wasn't exactly all we wanted it to be. Which, by the way, is a fantastic way to learn what you **do** want—by eliminating what you **don't** want! There are no mistakes.

But we do know how great it is to enjoy something, or to feel good about ourselves or a situation. It feels amazing, right? You must then believe you can have it and go on happily thinking about it even if it isn't here yet. If you get stuck, think about something else, something happy. Leave it alone for a while and don't worry. You do not need to think about it all the time for it to happen or manifest. You simply need to go about having a good life and finding joy in every possible moment. When you do that, your state of alignment will help you attract what you want. It won't likely happen overnight. It can happen quickly if you are aligned and wholeheartedly believing in your dreams, but often things show up when, or how, we least expect them. The absolute most important thing is to be happy now, be happy now, be happy now, even if the thing you want hasn't shown up yet.

Sometimes you figure out what you want when you notice something you don't want. If you focus on or keep repeating what you don't want, you can't attract what you do want. This is a biggie, so it is worth saying again in a different way to be sure you've got this.

Focusing on what you don't have, complaining, and just spewing negative language and thoughts into the atmosphere will not get you what you want. Hang in there with all of this. It gets easier with practice like anything else.

> **"THOUGHTS BECOME THINGS. CHOOSE THE GOOD ONES.®"**
> MIKE DOOLEY

CHAPTER TWO
Relationships

YOU, YOURSELF, AND YOU

Who are you?

Sometimes we believe we are who someone else says we are, and we think it is true. Has anyone ever said something to you like, "You are bad," or "You are so lazy," or "You are mean," and you believed it? It doesn't feel good when someone says something about a behavior in the moment and uses that to define **who** you are rather than what it really is: a temporary behavior on the path to learning and growing.

It goes something like this: 5-year old Sam is playing with his little sister Hannah who is 3. She has one of his trucks and won't give it back to him. Instead of just letting her have it for a while knowing she will be bored with it very soon, he does what most any 5-year old boy would do and gets madder and madder at her. And then he loses control and hits her over the head with his action figure. Of course, Hannah is in tears and Sam's dad is furious about it, telling Sam, "You are a bad boy." Sam's dad does not honestly believe that Sam IS a bad boy, but his behavior is not exactly a proud parent moment for him. Sam's behavior in that moment may be "bad," but Sam is **not** a bad person. Often adults just don't understand the potential long-lasting effect those types of statements can have on a kid. It is simply what they too were told as a kid by their well-meaning parents. So, if that has happened to you, understand that it is **not who you are** as a person, but how you were behaving in a learning moment and the parent, or whoever it was, just chose language that was not meant to define you as a bad person. Don't carry that with you through life, letting it define who you think you are. Let

it go, forgive them, forgive yourself, knowing it was a temporary, normal, learning moment.

So, **who are you?** Oh, so much more than can be put into words. You are part of all that is. You are love. You are worthy and here to experience all kinds of things. You are energy and light, here to learn, grow, expand, and find joy in it all, both the ups and the downs.

BEiNG SELF-iSH

Like most everyone you probably were taught at a young age not to be selfish, right? It is taught so that us wee little ones are nice to others and share and care about others, which is great and the way we want to be, of course. What ends up happening to most though, is that we grow up caring more about how others feel, how others feel about us, and what they think about us than how we ourselves

feel. Does that ever happen to you? Sometimes you end up doing things you don't want to do, like watching a TV program or playing a game you don't enjoy, so that you don't make someone else feel bad or mad, when all you want to do is listen to some music and doodle.

What we are talking about here is not a negative kind of selfishness. We are talking about positive self-care. When you are self-ish and care about how you feel more than anything else, you are respecting and honoring you, and you are of most benefit to everyone from that aligned state of being. We want to and should care about all others, but we are far better at being helpful to everyone and everything else when we care first about how we ourselves feel and our own alignment. We can make a great big positive difference in the world when we practice taking care of how we feel and being aligned first.

Lily

"It's good to be selfish! And I'm not talking about your money or the stuff you own. I'm talking about your emotions. Being selfish with emotions isn't something people talk about too often, but it plays a big role in how you feel. Here, I'll give you an example: Let's say you hear about a not so good situation happening with your friends, family or somewhere around the world. Something that you learn at an early age is to feel sad, depressed or angry about the situation. These feelings will cause your vibration to shift when you focus negatively on the problem. It's even worse when you feel bad about something you can't fix. So, I'm here to tell you there is something you can do: be selfish. You can send them your good thoughts or energy from in the vortex (in alignment). Law of Attraction says that thoughts become things. Putting a good thought their way will give you a sense of closure. You won't feel like you have to fuss over it. Also, it's good to keep in mind that bad things come and go, the things that are happening today aren't forever."

Trying not to join your friend in their suffering is going to be your best way to help them. If you can lift them up and help them feel hopeful, you are helping them in the best way possible.

Alone time

Are you thinking, "Wait a minute ... I thought we were talking about relationships here?" Well... we are. Consciously creating alone time, or self-time, is such a great gift to give yourself and the people who love you. We live in a busy world, and it sometimes seems that many people view busyness as a badge of honor, and they don't recognize the importance of alone time. We all want to be useful and valuable in life, right? Making time for time alone, and practicing alignment, is one of the best gifts you could give yourself.

YOUR INNER BEING

What is your inner-being? Your inner-being is your soul, who you really are, the child in you who was, and still is, sweet and innocent. The one who laughs and plays and only cares about how you feel and loving life, and everything and everyone in it. You are still that same energy and soul and forever will be. You can use this as a reminder during times when you forget who you really are and that life is supposed to feel good and you are here to experience joy and fun.

Role models

Do you have a role model? What are the characteristics about that person that are attractive to you? Are they kind, smart, funny, wise, talented in an area that you also love? Maybe they excel in a sport you love, maybe they have written a book, maybe they are an amazing guitar player or singer, maybe they have made a career as a cartoonist, a comedian, or a motivational speaker and you just love them! Why is that do you think? Perhaps your role model is modeling what your passion is and one day you hope to be your own version of that person? Yes, that is it! When you find someone who is living in a way that inspires you and you admire them, that likely is directing you toward some part of your passion and gift in life. Then you can choose the parts of what they do that feel great to you.

> **START COPYING WHAT YOU LOVE. COPY COPY COPY COPY. AT THE END OF THE COPY YOU WILL FIND YOUR SELF.**

YOHJI YAMAMOTO FROM *STEAL LIKE AN ARTIST* BY AUSTIN KELON (SEE HOW WE STOLE THAT?!)

When you find YOU in your copying, you will know you are acting and being authentically YOU! And nothing feels better than that! You have your own unique gifts and talents, and you are meant to use them.

SOMETIMES YOU
NEED TO BE ALONE.
NOT TO BE LONELY,
BUT TO ENJOY YOUR
FREE TIME
BEING YOURSELF.

Be nicer to your-self

Here is a story to help you better understand what using LOA to feel better about yourself looks like:

Old Story:

Molly stared at herself in the mirror and wondered what she could do about her nose, it was so thin and unattractive to her. "Maybe if I had a nice nose, Jake would ask me out. At least it would help my chances," she thinks. "I mean really, Kate has a cute nose, well a cute everything really, but her nose is really nice and mine ... isn't, and Kate has the attention of the cute guys all the time. She just laughs and smiles and it is so easy for her. Why is it so hard for me? And my eyes are so small and not a pretty blue like Kate's, mine are just plain and boring" she says as she stares at herself critically. "And my hair, well it is just ugly and the color is just so blah and it is not thick like Kate's and I don't know how to style it like she does hers. Why am I so hideous?" she thinks, as she gets angrier and angrier and throws her hairbrush across the bathroom floor, tears starting to flow. She stomps out of the bathroom and throws herself face down on her bed. "That's it," she thinks. "I am just ugly and no guy is ever going to like me. I feel so sad. That is how my life always goes, it is always that way, seriously it's just sad, and mad, and boring, and I am sick of it." She sighs heavily and blows her nose and heads to the kitchen for some chips and a soda to soothe herself. As she sits in front of the TV eating her chips and drinking her soda watching "America's Got Talent," she forgets about the pain. Ah, sweet relief ... for now.

As Molly wakes up the next morning, the first thought that comes into her mind is, "I hate school, I hate my life, this sucks, and I don't feel good." As she lies there, dreading school and thinking about how everything sucks, she starts to feel sick, thinking to herself, "My stomach does hurt, I mean it really hurts. Maybe I should stay home. Yeah, this isn't good, my head kind of hurts too. Am I hot?" She slooowwwwly drags herself out of bed and stumbles to the kitchen, shoulders slumped, where her parents are having breakfast, and croaks in a raspy voice, "I don't feel good." Her mom comes over and feels her forehead. "You aren't warm, maybe you should eat something first and see how you feel then," to which she replies, "I can't eat, I have a stomachache, and I feel like throwing up." "Well, ok then Molly," her mom says. "Go on up to bed, get some rest, and stay off your phone." And so there Molly lies, feeling more and more sick, restless, and bored as the day goes on.

New Story:

Molly stared at herself in the mirror and wondered what she could do about her nose, it was so thin and unattractive to her. "Maybe if I had a nice nose, Jake would ask me out. At least it would help my chances," she thinks. "I mean really" ... and she stops herself. She can feel a full-blown self-hate session coming on—she has done it many times before—so she takes in a deep breath and remembers what she has learned about thoughts becoming things and the laws of the universe. She realizes that she has gotten back into that negative self-talk pattern again, and she stops *herself right then and there and instead chooses to practice a different thought process in that instant.*

"Ok," she thinks as she looks on. "Is there anything about my nose that I can or do appreciate? Or do I just need to change the subject to something else and distract myself from the subject? Either way it is my choice, so here goes: Well, I guess it isn't a bad nose at all really, it is unique and strong. I don't hate it; it gives my face interest, actually. I've seen plenty of actresses with strong features as well and they are beautiful. I have high cheekbones and full lips. And I have great long legs, and they too are strong, and actually, come to think of it, I am strong and lean. I'm a healthy machine!" And to make her point to herself she does a high kick and a couple of jab punches into the air as she notices in the mirror how freakishly strong and able she is! "You've got this girl," she thinks to herself, as she runs down to the kitchen to grab an apple. Then she calls her friend Abby and asks her to ride to the park on their bikes. "It's a great day!" she thinks, as she heads out to meet Abby.

Hopefully that helps you better recognize when this kind of thing happens to you. You can see how in the old story, Molly ends up being negatively affected by her story, not only that day, but for the next day as well. The negative energy escalates. But the good news is, it doesn't have to. Once you shift to a positive energy that is your vibrational set point, you will feel the difference.

FRIENDS AND FOES?

Fitting in and being confident

Do you ever feel like you don't fit in? Maybe it doesn't happen often, and maybe it does, but everyone has felt that way at some point in life. What if it feels that way because a particular person or group isn't a good fit for you? Or maybe you don't even really have a "group" that you hang with. Or maybe you would like to hang out with a certain person or group but don't feel good enough in some way? When you focus on not fitting in, you have an energy about you that causes you to ... guess what! .... **not fit in**. Your energy isn't a match to your desire because it is matching what you **don't want** instead of what you **do want**, which is to fit in! We know, that part can be frustrating and challenging. Don't worry, find something that takes your focus off it and feels good, relax, and know you are perfect just the way you are. Just be you, because you do that best! There is nothing, we repeat, **nothing** wrong with you!

Lily

You don't need to fit in to be your confident self. You are you and nobody can take that away! If you think about how you don't fit in, you'll only bring more of that to you. So, do yourself a favor and think about happy things! What went good today? What's something you like about your personality or sense of style? Is there anything exciting coming up in the future? If you practice being happy in the moment, making peace and loving where you are, you will feel better and soon be in the habit of holding your head high and being proud of who you are. People will catch onto your high vibration and you will attract the right people to fit in with in your life.

How about practicing confidence instead? It *is* a practice. Try it sometime. Get yourself to a good feeling place, in alignment, as best you can. If you are beating yourself up or feeling angry because of a situation where you felt bad or if you are experiencing a negative emotion, you can get there. How? By doing something to feel good. Distract yourself in any way you can. Dance to your favorite song, shoot some hoops, or walk your dog. Or maybe it's just a good time to do something for someone else. You might be surprised, and so will your parents, at how good you feel when you do something, like emptying the dishwasher, picking up around the house, or offering to help your neighbor carry in her groceries, without anyone asking you or reminding you to do something. Learning how to feel good takes practice, especially if you have

practiced feeling bad or unworthy for a long time.

Once you've distracted yourself, and you are feeling aligned, imagine yourself in a situation where you feel confident. Role play it in your imagination. Use as much detail as you can and still feel good, then just enjoy the feeling of it. Aren't you smiling and feeling happy as you confidently interact with your friends? That is exactly what you want to practice again and again. You will become more and more comfortable with this imagined scenario, and your confident energy will soon show up in your real-life experience and not just your imagined one. Sweet!

FEELING LIKE A VICTIM

Are you feeling like a victim and just can't get to a better feeling place easily? Nobody wants to be mistreated or attracts being mistreated intentionally. You truly cannot control others. If someone is mistreating you, leaving you out, or doing something that causes you to feel bad, believe us, it isn't about you at all.

It's kind of like when someone has been picking on you in some way and you have a reaction. It may not even be a strongly noticeable reaction, but how you are feeling and your energy about it is clear to them. They have gotten the reaction from you they wanted, which makes them think they are powerful, which they don't actually feel. That is why they felt they had to find someone to take out their own powerlessness on and prove to themselves, and anyone watching, that they do have power.

Isn't it interesting that when one is mistreating another in some way, it is from a place of their own feeling of unworthiness or powerlessness? So, what can you do to keep them from choosing you?

If you choose to focus on how they are acting towards you, you too are operating from a misaligned energy vibration. There are things that you can do that won't get you in trouble and leave you feeling like a victim. Though it may not be easy to do at first, choosing distraction and not focusing on what has happened will be the best tool you can use to immediately raise your vibration. And the long-term benefit is that the other person will no longer be interested in interacting with you in that way. When you don't react, you raise your personal power and vibration. Positive energy always wins! You never, ever deserve to be mistreated by anyone, ever!!!!

So, what can you do from the standpoint of LOA? Try the following exercise and see if you find relief, and remember, learning LOA takes patience and practice.

EXERCISE // GOODBYE VICTIM

Step 1:

Sit in a comfortable place with a pen and paper.

Take a short time to write down what's bugging you.

Don't write a book about it, but just go there for a minute or two.

The intention of this exercise is to take those negative feelings, kiss them goodbye, and retrain how you think, how you feel, and therefore how you attract more positively.

Often just doing an exercise that physically makes you get rid of something undesired causes a shift in your thinking or perception, and therefore your attraction.

Now take that piece of paper and tear it up into tiny pieces.

Notice how you feel.

No emotion is wrong.

You can't get it wrong!!

Feel what you feel, and then, **STOP**.

Take those little pieces of paper and throw them in the garbage saying "Goodbye. You no longer have my attention or focus. Thanks anyway."

By doing this, you are choosing not to think about that situation again.

Step 2:

Get yourself into alignment.

Take several deep breaths.

Breathe in, saying "Present Moment."

Breathe out, saying "Happy Moment."

Do this five or six times or until you are feeling present, happy, and calm. That. Is. You!

The you that you were born to be. It is who you really are. You are eternally loved and adored. Honestly!!

Once you master this, you will even start to feel love for the person who was the one you felt victimized by.

That may seem hard to believe but it's true.

You will understand that this isn't about you, but about their own mis-alignment and lack of understanding of who they truly are.

It may take some time, but when your energy shifts from anger, fear, and worry to peace, calmness, worthiness, and love, those who seemed to bother you or were a problem to you before can't reach past your positive energy field and get to you so easily.

It is then that you know you truly have learned one of the most important lessons in life. It is a lesson that few truly master.

Pat yourself on the back please!

> **NOBODY CAN MAKE YOU FEEL INFERIOR WITHOUT YOUR CONSENT.**
>
> ELEANOR ROOSEVELT

Drama

Drama is simply a person's need to gain attention and a desire to have others believe as they do. If you choose (because you do get to choose) to be involved in others' drama you will likely have to pick sides. **Avoid it at all costs.** Change the subject, walk away, pretend you just swallowed a bug. Do all you can to avoid getting involved. It isn't helpful to anyone.

If a friend is in distress about her boyfriend who isn't paying attention to her, for example, and wants to talk with you about it, you've got to be able to separate yourself and not join in the anger, pain, or discomfort of it all. You cannot help them from that low energy vibration. If you can in any way uplift them, listen softly, without taking on their lowered vibration, or comfort them without getting yourself out of alignment, do so. If you cannot do so and you just feel it is too toxic for you and you can't help, do all you can to remove yourself from the situation. Tell them you care and you want them to be well and leave them lovingly for now. You will find a way to do it lovingly and with grace. Some things we just can't and shouldn't try to fix.

Using Empathy vs. Sympathy in the face of drama.

Empathy—Understanding their pain but not joining them in it. That way you can potentially bring them up to your high level. Now, time for fun!

Sympathy—Joining them in their pain. Now both of you are wallowing in the no-fun zone and just spinning in circles there. It is hard to get out. Now, sucky for all!

Peer Pressure

We all want to fit in, don't we? We want to be a part of what is going on and we don't want to experience FOMO (fear of missing out). So how do you stay cool and in the loop if others are doing things that your inner-being is saying no to, but your friends are wanting you to say yes to?

First, and most important, is to recognize that the gut feeling you have is your inner-being or intuition saying no to something you are being asked or pressured to do. It is giving you a signal to pass on doing that thing.

> **IF SOMETHING FEELS OFF, IT IS.**
>
> ABRAHAM HICKS

Old story:

Sam got off the bus to feel the warm sun on his face. He walked down to the school's front door, soon got to his locker and put his backpack inside, taking his science book out. "Sam!" he heard someone call from across the hall. He turned around to see his friend Connor waving and approaching him.

"Sam, me and a couple of other guys are leaving the school to go to the bowling alley. You should so come! It's going to be awesome!"

Sam looked at Connor who is smiling ear-to-ear. "You're ditching school? What about the English exam?" Sam had been studying for this for a while and he was confident that he was going to ace it. Not to mention English was his favorite subject, and he hoped to be a writer one day.

"We can just make it up later," Connor exclaimed.

"But if it's late, then that means we can't get more than a C on it."

"So?"

"So, I don't really want to have a C when I can easily have an A," Sam said.

Connor slumped his shoulders forward in defeat and then stood up straight again rolling his eyes. "You're such a bookworm. Who cares about the stupid test? Just come with us. It's much better than sitting in silence in an uncomfortable desk."

Sam considered leaving so he wouldn't have to hear Connor telling him how much fun he missed out on for weeks. "And it really does sound like fun," he thought. "Fine!" he finally said, pulling his backpack out of his locker and following Connor out of the school.

New Story:

Sam considered leaving so he wouldn't have to hear Connor telling him how much fun he missed out on for weeks. "And it really does sound like fun," he thought.

But, he hesitated, listened to his intuition, and knew what to do to feel good. "Dude, that would be cool, and so fun, but I'm going for an A here. Heck yeah, I need to be a bookworm if am going to be the one writing awesome best-selling books and making loads of money when I am done with all this school stuff. Thanks though for asking. Have an awesome time, and don't throw too many gutter balls. I will text you after school to see where you guys are and catch up with you then."

How does that story feel to you? Think about it, would you be upset with someone who chose a different activity than you, but did it in a positive and easygoing, fun way? Probably not, right? And if Connor was angry with Sam about it, that is his own guilt and misalignment that he has to deal with. The best part of that story is that Sam made an aligned decision for himself, and at the end of the day he will feel better for having chosen to do so, no matter what he might have "missed out on." He knows himself and trusts his intuition and guidance from his inner-being. That, friends, is what a superpower feels like!

Don't be jelly!

Jealously, or envy, doesn't feel good. It happens to everyone at some time in life. We see what another has, and we want it too, but we feel we will never have it or that we maybe aren't worthy of it in some way.

All of that kind of thinking is nonsense. You are worthy beyond measure. "Why don't I have those things then?"

you ask. There are a great many reasons, all of which are untrue or open for change. It is important to know that we all are here to experience life from a different vantage point. There is nothing wrong with you or your family or your circumstances. There is only opportunity for growth and expansion, as you attract whatever it is you do want in life. It's way hard to have a happy and attracting life if you are looking at what others have and what you currently don't. That is a sure way to attract more of the same.

When you notice someone living an experience you would like to have and you start to feel bad, simply note it as a potential desire that you would like to manifest in your life at some point and then do yourself a great big favor:

Change. The. Subject!

Old story:

Emma was going through the pictures on her social media feed only to see another amazing photo from Nicole's perfect life. Nicole was standing on a white sandy beach, holding a coconut. Emma thought, "It's not fair. Why am I stuck in the cold for winter-break when she's out there?" Emma went to Nicole's account to see more pictures of her smiling and looking perfect in every single photo, comparing the photos to her life, which to her seemed basic and bland. That's when she heard her mom knock on her door. "Hey honey, we're going out for sushi tonight. How much time do you need to get ready?"

"I'm not really up for sushi tonight," Emma said playing with her bracelet. Feeling the lump in her throat getting bigger. "I have a lot of homework. I think I'll stay home." She didn't have any homework but the last thing she wanted to do was be with other people. She felt sick.

"Okay, just make sure you eat something tonight. We'll see you when we get home." Emma's mom shut the bedroom door and soon Emma saw her family pull out of the driveway.

Emma spent the rest of the night sitting in her room looking through picture after picture. Making herself feel worse and worse with each one she saw, then falling asleep on her desk. She woke up to hear her family downstairs laughing and talking to one another. She looked at the time and it was only 8:30. She moved to her bed and pulled the covers to her chin. She heard her dad come in from her door behind her "Are you sleeping, Emma?"

She didn't reply. She then saw the lights in her room go out as he flipped the light switch and shut the door behind him.

New Story:

She heard her mom knock on her door. "Hey honey, we're going out for sushi tonight. How much time do you need to get ready?"

"Hmmm," she thinks. "Sushi?!" And she stops herself before responding, thinking, "I do love sushi. Am I going to sit here feeling sorry for myself, or am I going to walk away from viewing someone else's life and have a good time in my own?" "Sounds good," she says to her mom. "Can you give me five minutes—I just need to change?" "Yeah," she thinks, "I do need to change. Change my negative and self-defeating thoughts to better feeling ones. I may not be on a luxury vacation ... yet, but I know how to set myself up for that to happen another time. In the meantime, I am going to go out for some sushi and fun!"

The Three Sad Stooges: Negative, Pessimistic, & Gloomy

Whoever it is—a friend, family member, or a teacher—it isn't pleasant to be around negative energy. Whether we love them or barely know them, those negative ones can be a real pain, for sure. One thing is certain, they are not being happy, or aligned, with who they are. If they were, they wouldn't be acting the way they're acting.

What do you do when another person's energy is off? First of all, if your vibration is one of alignment, no matter what is going on, yours will be the dominant one. You will know by how you feel about a situation if your

energy is high or not. Be easy about it if you recognize that your vibration isn't up to speed. If you can remove yourself from the other's energy, do so, and either way find any thought you can that feels better than the one you are feeling, or being surrounded by, in that moment. It takes some practice, but it is worth choosing a better feeling thought in these moments, because it will give you a sense of peace. When you get really good at it, others will also benefit from your high-flying energy and will actually be drawn to you because you make them feel good, simply because **you feel good, no matter what is going on**. That is powerful!! Give it a try!

And remember, it is their story, not yours. You are not here to make anyone else happy. Only they can do that for themselves. Lovingly, and energetically, place them outside your positive energy field. And smile, because you are glad you know this information.

Those negative ones are just frustrated and unhappy with themselves at the core of it all. So, try to avoid joining in and participating in their misery. Try to be neutral and keep your energy out of that pit. If you join them where they are, you are lowering your own energy flow. You get to choose.

> **BE THE KIND OF FRIEND YOU WANT TO MEET.**

When your energy is high, you will not attract these negative people anyway. You may also notice and want to check in with your own energy because sometimes you are the one in a negative place and the positive energy one is annoying to you. If that is so, join them up there and have fun!

When it comes to friends, choose ones that feel good to hang with, instead of the ones that don't.

FAMILY DYNAMICS

Parents and Expectations – What do you want from me?

Even though you already know it, sometimes it may seem hard to believe that your parent/parents love you. Even if how they are acting or treating you makes you think otherwise. They do want what's best for you and are trying their best, in the only way they know how to guide you and take care of you. Parents aren't perfect, but no matter what, they love you more than you could imagine. Sometimes parents feel like big kids in adult costumes. They make mistakes and sometimes feel overwhelmed too. Be patient with them, communicate with them. They are learning and do-ing their best to be good parents. We never stop learning.

What parents want is for you to be happy. They also want you to be successful. They want you to be, do, and have, better than they did or do. Shhh... don't tell them, but you did not come here to please your parents. You came here for your own individual experience, as they did. Love them, do what you need to do, and make it as enjoyable as possible.

If you go about life looking for things that are pleasing to you, even if your parents, the adults, aren't living in their happy place, and you still choose feeling good, you are, and will continue to be successful! Sweet, huh?!

Divorce

Nobody wants to go through a divorce, not you, and not your parents either. It is especially challenging if you feel pulled one way or another, or you feel stuck in the middle of it all.

It is a hard time for everyone that is for sure. So, what can you do to remain neutral and loving to both of your parents if you are feeling stuck in the middle and feeling like you have to choose sides?

First it is important to understand that it isn't up to you to fix anything for them. This is their own journey. The very best thing you can do is to practice your own alignment first and trust that everything will work out in time. It may not be super easy to do that in the middle of things, but it will be the best thing you can do, so it is worth noticing how you are feeling and then doing all you can to shift to better feeling thoughts when you catch yourself in a downward swing of emotion.

If one parent in particular is in emotional distress, and is deeply hurt, you will be of most benefit to them to approach them, and love them, when you feel as positively aligned as you can be under the circumstances. You can uplift them best by not joining them in their distress even though it can feel like you want to sympathize with them in the moment. Can you imagine how great it would feel to be able to uplift a parent when they are feeling down? Pretty awesome, right?!

Story:

> Zach's parents have split up and are going through a divorce. He is splitting his time with his parents, living primarily with his mother and spending every other weekend with his father. His mother feels hurt and angry and though she doesn't mean to make things more difficult for Zach, she complains to him about his father often and

questions him after he has spent time with his father. He feels uncomfortable about it, but he doesn't know what to do. He wants to help his mom feel good, and he loves both of his parents, so what can he do that keeps himself aligned, he wonders? And he decides to practice what he has been learning about positive energy, and feeling the best he can, even in difficult situations. He knows that his alignment can also be helpful to both of his parents, and since that is what he also wants, it feels like his best choice of action.

He has just returned from a weekend at his father's and he knows that his mom will be home soon, so he decides to crank up some tunes and do some push-ups and kick boxing to release some energy and get some endorphins flowing to help even out his anxiousness and tension. By the time he is done, he is feeling more relaxed. Good start, he thinks. Then he decides to practice the conversation he wants to have with his mom since he is feeling pretty good.

He imagines a conversation that is loving and kind. He thinks about how he will lovingly move the conversation in a positive direction and change the subject in a kind manner if it goes in a negative direction. He can hear himself kindly sharing how he feels with her, and he can see her soften and come to understand his message. He can visualize the positive result of the conversation very clearly in his mind and it feels great. He has learned that this tool gives him the best chance of having the kind of conversation that feels great to both of them.

He hears his mom coming in the door. He takes a deep calming breath, smiles, and heads in to greet her. As she sees his warm smile, her energy also shifts to a softer place, (Positive energy always wins) and he knows that their interaction is going to be good. And he is right!

Question: What if Zach gets himself into alignment and his mother still doesn't soften, or worse, is angrier than ever?

He will have to understand that he cannot control her emotions. He can only control his own. Though it isn't easy to watch that happening to someone he loves and lives with, he must do all he can to avoid picking up her burden. That is not his responsibility and isn't helpful to either of them.

Sibling rivalry

It certainly happens, doesn't it? You love your brother(s) and/or sister(s), but they can drive you crazy like nobody else can! Grrrrrrr!!!!

With siblings, it most often begins with feelings of jealousy and frustration about the other. One feels that the other is treated better, loved more, is smarter, better in sports, funnier, and just better overall. Sometimes it seems like they just have a desire to irritate you for no apparent reason. It may be that they see something of themselves in you. Like, some habit or behavior they don't much like and it irritates them, or they feel jealous of something you are good at or do well. They know your trigger points, as you know theirs. And they like to get you to react and shake things up a bit.

However, it isn't about you. They are acting out because of who they are and how they are feeling. You are the easiest prey for them because you are close by and you react. This doesn't mean they hate you or are mean-spirited. They are just out of touch with who they are, and you are their closest target. And the same is true when you treat them that way. Hey, don't beat yourself, or them, up about it. Hang in there. This too shall pass! Take a walk, turn on some tunes, watch a funny video, do whatever you can to raise your energy level and see what happens.

If you have a sibling, or siblings, and you feel as if you would rather that they move to China or Bora Bora, just know that this is an important relationship for you. It is one that teaches you how to be in future relationships. You are each uniquely and beautifully created, and you came to be here together to learn and share this special bond. Go ahead and irritate, be irritated, and love, knowing and appreciating these bonds, understanding that the only thing that matters is your alignment, actions, and reactions to them. Choose good ones.

If you have no siblings, you came here to learn from a different perspective. And that is a great thing as well! We all came here for different reasons and to experience life in different ways. There are no mistakes.

TEACHERS, COACHES, BOSSES, PREACHERS

This section is focused on teachers and coaches, but it relates to anyone in life who is a leader, guide, or mentor who is there to teach you something.

Teachers

Lily

"Teachers are often hard to have a good vibration towards considering they are the giver of homework. We all have that teacher who teaches like they are purposely trying to make you fall asleep on your desk or who assigns so much homework you're up till 2 o'clock in the morning learning about triangles. No matter what it is, it may get you ticked off. Something that you may not think about is seeing them as a human. I know what you're thinking WHAT!? Teachers are human!? Yes, I know! was surprised to hear that too, and they most likely have gone into education for you, the student. They do these horrible things to make sure you get a good understanding of the things you are learning. See things from their perspective. They don't do it because they are evil lizard people, they do it so you get the best out of your learning career."

Coaches

If you are involved in a sport maybe you are feeling the pressure of participating and keeping up with all of it and performing in a way that pleases your coach, as well as your parents. And though you like your sport, you sometimes wonder why you are doing it, or you feel pressured to do it, or you have to do it for one reason or another.

Of course, you want to be great at what you are doing. If you aren't performing as well as you would like, you may be very hard on yourself. If you're not performing as well as your coach would like, and your coach is hard on you, it doesn't feel good. Or maybe you have a parent who gets frustrated with you about your performance or puts extra pressure on you to excel in the sport.

So, what are your choices?

· Have a conversation with your coach and/or parents to find out what your options are or tell them how you are feeling.

· Make a decision to stick with it, enjoy it, and make the best of it.

· Decide that it is in your best interest to choose not to participate next season, and just do your best this season.

· Decide, even if you're feeling pressure, to simply do your best, have fun, and know that you don't have to please anyone.

· Choose to continue with the best possible energy, because, right now, choosing to stay and play feels far better than leaving and facing the repercussions or negative feelings you might have after doing so.

· If you just feel you must leave the team, consider how would that would make you feel.

· Or (please don't choose this one!) continue to feel stress and pressure about it.

None of the decisions are wrong, not even the last one. That one is just the most difficult path to take. The options are unique to you and your situation, and no matter what choices you do or do not have at this moment, you are free to choose the joyful path, in any circumstance. Be easy on yourself. Do your best, practice being relaxed and easy, and appreciate the lessons in all of it. Life is for learning and growing. You are making decisions at every turn. You have more choices than you think. Let how you feel guide you.

Really, what is the worst thing that can happen if you don't play well? Will the world come to an end? Will it matter in the big picture of your life? Not likely, so do whatever it is, in fun, and don't take anything too seriously. It's a game. ~ Have FUN!

DATING

For those of you who are of dating age, this information is for you. For those of you who are younger, this section is also beneficial in dealing with friendships.

I'm not that into you— being rejected

Being rejected doesn't feel good that is for sure. It is painful, and it happens to everyone at some point in life, not just when dating someone, but we are also sometimes rejected by friends. It's a drag and it hurts, so how do you carry on with the least amount of agony?

Like with everything that happens, or that we create in life, we get to choose how we will operate and think moving forward. It doesn't make it painless, nor does it make everything go away. As always, in challenging and difficult situations, it is most helpful to remember that it is an opportunity for growth, and creating new desires for improvement in future relationships or events.

Sure, feel sad, or angry, and cry if you need to, and get it out. It's perfectly ok to feel all of that. Then, when you are ready to feel better, do all that you can, not to think about it even though that isn't always easiest thing to do. Look at what you learned from it or choose to think about the new opportunities that might arise out of the situation. Do all you can to not carry it around with you now, like a bag of weights, so you don't drag that heavy burden into your future. He or she has moved on, and so shall you. Realize that you deserve to be treated like you would like to be treated and to have what you want in a relationship. Your future relationships will be full of new opportunities for you, and with time it won't hurt so much, we promise. Spend a little time to redefine what it is you want in a future boyfriend/girlfriend (or friend), and then take a breather. Do something nice for yourself and for someone else. Don't be in a hurry. Take care of you, now. Process what you need to process and try not to hang out in Sadville, listening to sad songs, too long. Do yourself a favor and find a positive friend to talk to, watch a funny movie, or grab some earbuds and listen to some feel-good tunes.

Maybe you can turn this situation into something positive. Ever notice how singers produce some really great music after a breakup? They redirect their energy and make millions!

Pressure and respecting boundaries

Don't do anything you aren't ready for or in alignment with. The only person who should ever decide when, or what, you are ready for is you. Your inner-being, gut instinct, or intuition will always tell you if something is a

YOUR INNER BEING
IS ALWAYS
GUIDING YOU.

LISTEN TO IT.

good choice, and an aligned decision for you, and you will know by listening and paying attention to how you feel.

You know that little voice inside of you that says, "Hmmm, maybe I shouldn't do this"? That is your inner-being, letting you know that you are not connected to who you really are in that moment. If there is a feeling of uncertainty, it is certain you are not ready for what is being suggested. When you know that, you can say "No, thank you," and you will not later regret making a choice that you weren't ready for or wanting. Standing up for yourself always looks beautiful and feels good.

There is a difference between doing something scary for the first time, like learning to swim underwater or learning to ride a bike or taking your first airplane ride, and doing something that just doesn't feel right to you or right for you. Your inner-being is telling you. It is just something you have to pay attention to in order to make a choice that is right for you and one you won't regret later.

Lily

I see my inner-being as Lily (me) but a version of me that is cooler, wiser, and unconditionally joyous. If I'm ever in a predicament I just think, "Hmmmm... what would lily do?" I like thinking about it this way because a lot of the times I am that version of me and it truly feels amazing when I am! It almost feels like I'm walking on stilts, the world seems vibrant and alive.

Relationships aren't always easy, but we came here to interact with all kinds of people. We are all here together, experiencing all kinds of things, wanted and unwanted. The entire world is one big relationship, energetically speaking, and we all came to share the experience together, and have fun along the way.

CHAPTER THREE
Thoughts and Beliefs

WHAT ARE YOU THINKING?

Everything is energy. We have said this more than once, but it is totally worth repeating.

Your thoughts matter in attracting what you want in life. The great thing about thoughts, is that you can learn to shift them anytime you desire, and the more you make them positive, the more positive outcomes you attract and see in your life. Want a happy life? Think happy thoughts. It really is that easy. It can be the simplest things like, "I am not deaf, I can hear birds sing," or "I am not blind, I can see the sunset," or "I have legs, I can walk my awesome Cakewalk, or run like the wind," as long as it feels good to you, and increases your power as a "Magician of manifestation!"

Sure, there are times and things that are difficult, and you will have times

of pain and sadness. That is a normal and important part of life as well. It is more important to see those challenging times as times of growth and opportunity. If we didn't know sadness, we couldn't know happiness.

You are free to think and imagine whatever you wish. And by choosing either positive or negative thoughts you ultimately get to decide how you will live your life.

LETTING GO OF THE LITTLE THINGS

Do you ever notice how something that isn't really a BIG deal grabs your attention and focus and can put you in a mood that isn't so positive? It may cause you to worry or overthink and it

seems like you literally can't let it go. It is understandable and happens sometimes, but when you practice getting aligned and get good at changing the subject, you will notice that negative emotions showing up less and less. And when those situations do show up, it almost seems like a game. You will catch it before it becomes the big monster that it used to, and you will feel ease and relief settle in. That is when you feel the awesome power of being in touch with who you really are. You will also feel a great sense of freedom when you understand that you can control your emotions so well.

Lily

Thinking positive or negative thoughts is really all about habits. This past year I really learned about how much thoughts can affect you and how they change the way you feel. I also picked up on how to stop the negative thoughts from taking over my emotions. I've been working on how to be ok with the negative situations that come up in my day-to-day life, and how to move on from these things. I simply tell myself that bad situations come and go, then do my best to move onto a new subject that makes me feel good.

For a while I got into the habit of giving myself worried thoughts. Like, "Oh no! Did that person think that was weird?" or "Did I forget about the math homework?!" I held onto those little things for too long worrying about the what if's! I soon enough realized my bad habit and did my best to fix it. Of course, I slip up here and there, but I sure am on my way to feeling more at ease!

"Tell me what you want, what you really, really want!"

Start your sentences with "I want" and state what you desire, instead of starting with "I don't want." When you state what you do want you are starting to attract it; when you state what you don't want you are doing the same. What do you want to attract?

Saying "No" statements

"I don't like school"

"Why can't I throw a football like Drew?"

"I don't want to take the test"

Saying "Yes" statements

"I like Ms. Madsen, my art class, and seeing my friends every day"

"I can out-run most of my class."

"I'll feel great when I finish this test."

It is helpful to define what you don't want, so that you know what you do want. Just don't hang out there repeating your "No" statements and attracting what you don't want. Just say "Yes"!

Taking action:

When you stay in the flow of life just enjoying and paying attention to how you feel, you will be inspired to take the actions that help you to get what you want. You will have doors open that you wouldn't have been able to see when you were focused on what you don't want. Magic starts happening.

EXERCISE // TAKING ACTION

Grab a pen and paper and write down a statement that you maybe have said or thought about recently or something that you don't want. Now, cross out that statement and turn the page over.

Now set that aside and close your eyes and relax. Take some deep breaths and get yourself aligned and feeling good. When you feel peaceful and aligned, open your eyes.

Grab your pen and paper again and on the top of the blank page write down the first positive thoughts or words that come to you.

Now, for the next 5 or 10 minutes, tell a better feeling story than the one you originally told. Try to get some positive momentum going and notice how you feel shifts and positive momentum builds. This is an exercise that is setting you up for having what you desire in life. Even the smallest improvement is of great value to you and your attracting energy.

Your Emotions

Your emotions are your indication of alignment or misalignment:

Misalignment	Alignment
Fear & Worry	Peace
Anger & Frustration	Ease
Hate	Love
Jealousy	Acceptance
Sadness	Happiness
Guilt	Self-Love
Doubt	Hope
Stress	Freedom

Don't worry about your emotions and feel that you have to control them in every waking moment. Sometimes you will feel negative/misaligned emotions. It is a normal part of life. Wouldn't it feel great to know that feeling down is not a bad thing? The mastery of it all is learning to notice that emotion, accept it as the learning emotion it is, and then calmly let it go. Once you learn to focus on positive thoughts, you will catch the negative emotions/misalignment quicker and have less of those types of experiences. It is SO cool, and you can't unlearn alignment!!

STRESS—SCHOOL, HOMEWORK, AND SPORTS

We've heard about this from many of you we've talked to, as well as from your parents. For you, homework and sports, may be the two areas of life where you constantly feel stressed. So, what can you do with that?

Maybe it is just that you don't feel that you have enough time to do it all, or that you have to put one activity before the other. Perhaps you feel pressured by a coach to prioritize your sport, or parents want you to do, or be great, in all of it. Maybe it just feels boring or unexciting to you. Whatever it is that stresses you out, know that you are not alone and that by making some small shifts in thinking, you can start to feel better about it and attract more ease and flow with it. When you get good at alignment and don't take any of it too seriously, stress goes down. Give it time. Sound good? Heck Yeah!

Lily's own story:

"School was always a struggle for me. It wasn't interesting to me and it was difficult to understand the things we were learning. My worst class, by far, was math. I thought that it was absolutely pointless to learn what the difference between an acute and an obtuse angle was. Homework was a nightly struggle for me to finish. Most nights resulting in tears.

Fast forward to 8th grade. The year I stopped doing my homework most nights because I wanted to do other things, like hang out with friends and chill. But the homework didn't simply disappear like I hoped it would, it just piled up, and The Big Fat F in the gradebook was in my thoughts most of my day. I didn't have any of my grades above a C, not even in my favorite class, which was art. The end of the year was right around the corner, and it wasn't looking pretty. Finally, it got to the point where the school had to bring in my parents and we had to talk to the guidance counselor. She told me that if my grades stayed where they were when the year ended they would have to hold me back. My parents and I made a plan of action, and I talked to my teachers to find a way to get my grades up from an F. After a lot of stress and anxiety, I got my Fs up to Ds. Just enough to pass that year.

I was aware of the law of attraction and what it was, but over the summer before the 9th grade, I really figured out how to use it, and when the school year was right around the corner, I decided that I was going to kick school's butt. I did exactly that: I did well in all my classes, it was easy for me to understand, and now a year later my worst class has become the easiest for me. I am in 10th grade now and I'm in an advanced class this year, which is something I would have never thought possible a couple years ago. It's all because I decided that it was going to be easy for me, I changed the way I thought about school and grades. I am easy about it now and remind myself that it's all going to work out well for me no matter what."

———————————————

When Lily decided and committed to doing better for herself, without resistance, that is exactly what she did! Better ~ A whole lot better, in fact! Give that girl an "A" for Alignment!

So then, let's talk about homework. Can you say stress?! If you have an assignment that is due tomorrow and you decide not to do it, how does that feel? Which would feel better tomorrow: having it done or choosing not to do it? Choosing not to do it now isn't going to feel very good tomorrow, right? You know from experience, if you have ever not gotten an assignment done, it feels pretty stressful. So, wouldn't it feel so much better if you were to think about tomorrow, and just decide, right then, to get at it, and get it done? Like Nike says, "Just Do It" and remind yourself of how much happier you will be having gotten it done! Would you feel a sense of ease and relief? Most likely! Less stress = more fun!

Some things regarding school and sports feel out of your control, right? Sure, you do have things you need to do to graduate, or practice and master a skill, or compete in your chosen sport. The part you do have complete control of is how you are going to choose to feel about what it is you are being required to do, to have the outcome you want. Unless you don't want to, or care to graduate, or do well in your sport, of course. Then you are choosing a different path, but again, you choose it.

The best, and most useful way to eliminate or lessen your feelings of stress is to view it from that perspective. Look at the bigger picture and decide that doing the thing, without resistance, is far less stressful than you were making it out to be.

These are the tools you will use for preventing future stress as well! You will have the gift of warding off undue stress as an adult, if you learn to manage it at your age. This superpower will set you free and guide you every step of the way. We are fist bumping you here! Boom!

Sadness

If you are generally healthy and happy, and yet sometimes you just feel down, depressed, sad, anxious, worried, or fearful, know that it isn't a bad thing at all. It is contrast that helps us in defining what we want and is what makes the highs feel higher. It is supposed to be that way. Taking those occasional dips in our emotions is normal and healthy. What do you do when you just can't seem to get into alignment? Don't beat yourself up and really, just be easy about it, knowing that in time, with practice, you will get unstuck faster and faster. Say things to yourself that make you feel even just a little better.

Practice gratitude. Make a list of 10 things you are grateful for. Anything ranging from the book you are reading, and the ability to read it, to someone who is important to you in your life, to the beautiful tree in your backyard that you have climbed or sat under so many times.

Smiling helps everything. If you just can't get out of it, watch a funny video. Anything to make you laugh will release some much-needed endorphins in your system and make it easy to move to a better feeling place.

P.S. Moving your body is highly encouraged here! Even simple things like stretching, taking a walk, touching your toes, dancing, hopping on your bike. Test yourself. See how many jumping jacks, push-ups, or squats you can do.

Whatever you choose to do, don't feel bad about feeling bad. The universe has your back, and so do we.

With Love, sending you positive energy vibes!

In a funk

How would you feel if you knew that being in a funk is a normal thing and is actually a period of growth and improvement? Kind of refreshing, right? We certainly don't view it that way in our society, do we?

Dalaney was having a few bad days in a row. She was in a slump and a funk and she knew it. But she couldn't quite see how to get herself out of it. She wondered if there was something wrong with her and she was trying to analyze what it was. She knew some LOA, but feeling the way she did, she couldn't quite grasp a good feeling thought. She was stuck feeling down, down, down. Until she got real tired of it, and then remembered that it was ok to feel that way for a while and that "unfunking" herself was up to her. She decided right then and there to get out and do something about it. She knew she needed to change the subject. It wasn't as hard as she was letting it be for the past few days. She decided to call her friend Mia, thinking how funny it was that she was avoiding everyone to hang in blah, and that simply calling a positive friend to chat would start the momentum towards feeling better and better. She then did a little dance party to "Uptown Funk" and raised her energy level even more! By the next day she was feeling like her awesome self again!

It was when she got to the other side of it, that she realized the power she had, and how absolutely great she felt after feeling so cruddy. It's contrast and it helps clarify what you want and what you don't want.

Practice these statements, or create your own list that feels good to you:

This too shall pass.

I don't have to have all the answers right now.

It's gonna be alright – It IS alright.

I don't need to try so hard.

I'm not weak–I am strong.

I'm not getting it wrong–there is no "wrong."

I'll feel better soon–I'm feeling better already.

I am powerful.

I love myself.

I am normal.

In fact, sometimes I'm pretty awesome!

Sometimes, well mostly, I am the bomb!

_____

_____

_____

Listening to your intuition

Intuition – What does it mean?

Intuition is really a cool thing. Intuition is really guidance from God/Source/The Universe. The definition is: "the ability to understand something immediately, without the need for conscious reasoning" or "a thing that one knows or considers likely from instinctive feeling rather than conscious reasoning."

You know how sometimes you can almost hear your inner-voice telling you what to do? Listen to it. That is your inner-guidance system, your true-self at work telling you what you need to

know, and helping you make wise decisions that are best for you and will bring you the greatest happiness and success in life.

Imagination

> **THE IMAGINATION, THE SCISSORS OF THE MIND, IS CONSTANTLY CUTTING OUT THE EVENTS TO COME INTO YOUR LIFE.**
>
> *THE SECRET DOOR TO SUCCESS*, FLORENCE SCOVEL SHINN

To use your imagination is like using a scissors cutting out a picture for your life and how you want it to be. Your imagination is a great tool for creating the things and events you wish to see in your life.

EXERCISE //
"SCISSORS OF THE MIND"

A great exercise to help you see what you imagine even more clearly, is to create a vision board.

To do this you simply find pictures of things you want to experience or have, cut them out, and glue them onto a piece of poster board, foam core, or anything you have access to.

Then you use your imagination to see yourself joyfully doing or having that thing.

As long as you feel good while doing this and are not feeling the absence of it, your desire is on it's way.

You have literally cut out the images from "the scissors of the mind" and glued them right in front of you to view each day!

BELIEVE IT AND YOU WILL SEE IT

What are beliefs?

Beliefs are just thoughts you have practiced for a long time. If we practice anything long enough it becomes what we call our reality. And then you see evidence all around you to support that belief, that you've created, by your practiced thoughts about it.

You've probably heard people say, "I'll believe it when I see it." It seems reasonable to think that's the way it works, but once you understand the laws of the universe you realize that it is the other way around. If you need to see the evidence before you believe it, it cannot come, at least not easily. How is that working out for you?

Let's say you want a new bike but there is an inner voice inside you saying, "Yeah right, like that is going to happen."

That is a resistant vibration or thought pattern that will keep it from showing up. You might put forth effort to change that thought saying, "I deserve it" or "If Tyler can have one, so can I," but these thoughts also have resistance, or negative emotion, in them that will most likely keep that bike from being parked in your driveway anytime soon.

However, if you can ask or put the intention out for the new bike when you are aligned and in tune, you move about in life feeling good, you believe it, and don't measure where it is or when it is coming. You are essentially getting out of the way and letting it come to you.

> **HAPPY NOW, HAPPY NOW, HAPPY NOW.**
> ABRAHAM HICKS

WHAT IF YOU DON'T GET WHAT YOU WANT?

This usually means that you are not ready for that yet and maybe you are spending time measuring or worrying about where it is and not living happy now. It is on its way, but you are slowing it down by focusing on it not being here. Try letting it go, get happy, and know that it is coming. If you think about the new bike and it feels great and exciting and does not trip you up, you know you are in alignment with it. If you feel frustrated that it isn't here yet, you likely won't be seeing it anytime soon. And if that is the case, your best option is to change the subject to something that feels good.

If you are saving your money to buy it yourself, you have action to take to actually have enough cash to bring it to you. So, practice feeling good when you are earning the money and saving up the money for it.

Feeling good is all that matters; no kidding! Do you "deserve" it? Of course, you do. Believe that! We all are deserving of wonderful experiences and things, and as long as we aren't putting resistance on our path that trips us up, we can live the wonderful experiences we came here for.

WHAT OTHERS BELIEVE

What others are thinking can affect you either positively or negatively, if you don't pay attention to how it makes you feel. It sometimes sneaks in so quietly you may not notice it. Don't believe everything you hear.

For instance, let's say that Allie believes that everyone on the cheer squad is stuck up. She constantly talks about her belief, tells you about it, you agree, and you both see it happen again and again. You've let her beliefs become yours, and now you even see evidence to support it. Then, you can both be "right" and talk about it and see more and more of it.

But, when you understand energy, and you don't engage in and share her belief, you won't see the others on the cheer squad as being stuck up, but instead you may start to see them as really nice people. It's ok— Allie is just practicing what she has learned and what comes easiest for most. She doesn't know about the power of positively aligned energy ... yet. Maybe you will teach by your example. You don't have to agree with someone to be his or her friend. You can love that person and still be friends without getting on board with their beliefs. Even if you just have to smile and send them positive energy without making a comment. Or better yet, you could say that you haven't noticed that at all, and that in fact one of the members of the cheer squad is in your history class, and she is super sweet. Do whatever you can not to go there with the other person's beliefs and change the subject if at all possible. Believe in the goodness of everyone and make every day fun. Watch out, you may become a total fun-magnet!

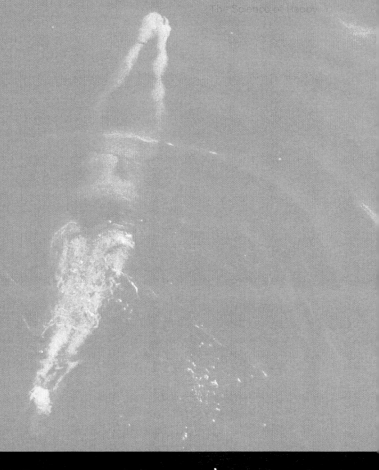

IF YOU BELIEVE YOU CAN, OR YOU CAN'T, YOU ARE RIGHT.

HENRY FORD

CHAPTER FOUR
It's Your Life

WHY AM I HERE?

Do you ever wonder that? The answer is simple: You are here to experience expansion.

You are here for the joy of it all.

You are here to have fun, learn, be adventurous, feel excited, make lots of mistakes, experience sadness, to give, and receive love, and most of all, to feel happy in the mix of it all.

YOUR FUTURE

> **WHEN I WAS 5 YEARS OLD, MY MOTHER ALWAYS TOLD ME THAT HAPPINESS WAS THE KEY TO LIFE. WHEN I WENT TO SCHOOL, THEY ASKED ME WHAT I WANTED TO BE WHEN I GREW UP. I WROTE DOWN 'HAPPY.' THEY TOLD ME I DIDN'T UNDERSTAND THE ASSIGNMENT, AND I TOLD THEM THEY DIDN'T UNDERSTAND LIFE.**

JOHN LENNON

"Whatcha' gonna do?"

You probably have been asked more than once, "What do you want to be, or do, when you grow up?"

While people mean well in asking, and certainly you will want to have an idea of what direction you might go by the

time you graduate from high school, it doesn't necessarily serve you best to decide exactly **"what"** you want to be, but more beneficial to first ask yourself **"how"** you want to be, and then you will better be able to decide what you will do that supports how you want to feel in life.

HOW DO YOU WANT TO BE, OR FEEL, WHEN YOU GROW UP?

Do you see yourself happy and doing work you love? Are you feeling fulfilled? Inspired? Excited? Adventurous? Grateful? Or all of the above?! Yes! Then you are better able to move towards doing things that support **"how"** you want to be.

Let's say you love sports. You love everything about sports, you lose track of time when you are engaged in what is going on in the field, or on the court, etc. Maybe you love to talk

about it. Maybe you have a gift for remembering stats. Maybe you have a strong understanding of certain aspects of the game that others don't see. Maybe you think being a sportscaster or a coach or something sports related would be a dream come true. Maybe you will work in the stadium in some capacity.

Or, maybe you love fashion. You design outfits in your head or on paper all the time. You can see your designs on the runway. You want to learn so much more.

Maybe you want to be a doctor or a nurse. Maybe you want to build things. Maybe you want to drive a truck, be an accountant, do landscaping, be a hairstylist, be the president, or fly to the moon. You get to choose.

Maybe you have **NO** idea, and that is perfectly ok too.

You won't make a wrong decision if you move in a direction that feels good to you. Maybe you will have a job that isn't your dream job, as you work towards your dream career or hobby. It's important to remember that you can't make a mistake in choosing a path.

As you go through life, you will figure out what feels good, as well as what you don't much care for, and then make decisions that lead you toward work that is fulfilling. The most important thing is to have fun all along the way. Often people start careers or jobs that lead them to what it is they truly desire. We are forever changing, growing, and expanding—thank goodness!

You might have heard people say, "Ice Cream: Vanilla or Chocolate?" and you choose one. When you are faced with a decision, choose what feels best to you and know that it is the best choice, no matter what.

> A VERY GOOD CAREER CHOICE WOULD BE TO GRAVITATE TOWARD THOSE ACTIVITIES AND TO EMBRACE THOSE DESIRES THAT HARMONIZE WITH YOUR CORE INTENTIONS, WHICH ARE FREEDOM AND GROWTH—AND JOY. MAKE A CAREER OF LIVING A HAPPY LIFE RATHER THAN TRYING TO FIND WORK THAT WILL PRODUCE ENOUGH INCOME THAT YOU CAN DO THINGS WITH YOUR MONEY THAT WILL THEN MAKE YOU HAPPY. WHEN FEELING HAPPY IS OF PARAMOUNT IMPORTANCE TO YOU—AND WHAT YOU DO FOR A LIVING MAKES YOU HAPPY—YOU HAVE FOUND THE BEST OF ALL COMBINATIONS.

ABRAHAM-HICKS

Seriously

Society often tells us that we have to get serious in order to be successful and have a happy life. You can have a happy life, no matter what you are doing, and being "serious" about it mostly causes problems.

The synonyms for serious are: solemn, earnest, grave, somber, sober, unsmiling, stern, grim, humorless. Sounds Un-Fun doesn't it?

Sure, there is action to take in life, but hopefully you will choose the most fun and enjoyable path. You can have fun cleaning toilets if you have the right attitude. It is when you focus on, and take action on, something that feels exciting to you that you are setting yourself up for a happy and fulfilling life experience.

Imagine yourself doing something you love doing and hold that vision of you doing that thing. If it feels really good you are on the right track. Move in that direction and know that no matter what you choose, it isn't wrong.

Let's say that again: no matter what you choose, it isn't wrong!

Everything we experience can be a learning experience that moves us either toward what we do want or what we don't want and then we can change direction towards what we want.

Don't worry if you are strongly encouraged, pushed, or shoved, by others who love you, and mean well, in another direction, and you don't exactly get to choose it right now. Do what you need to do, enjoy whatever that is, and see what happens! You can still hold and create a dream that you are moving towards. At some point, you will get to choose exactly what you want, and your desires will always flow and change. That is a great thing! Embrace change, growth and expansion!! You can't get it wrong, and you never get it done. While you are here on earth you will always want something. It is why you came here.

> **YOU CAN'T GET IT WRONG, AND YOU NEVER GET IT DONE.**
> ABRAHAM-HICKS

How do you want to feel?

Once you decide how you want to feel in life and you lean in that direction, doing things that make you lose all sense of time, and you keep practicing that, you will likely start to see paths that your passion can take you. Maybe it will just be a hobby that you love, or maybe a career path will unfold for you that is wildly fulfilling and shows you how you want to feel and engage in life.

Each and every one of you have much to offer the world! Just be easy about all of it and do what you do and be **HOW** you want to be, and things will unfold for you like magic. Don't take any of it too seriously or you will miss the point and the joy of life itself. Appreciate the mistakes, misdirections, and failures, knowing that they are just moving you to the next wanted thing!

EXERCISE //
HOW DO YOU WANT TO FEEL?

Start making a list of how you want to feel in life.

Happy, Strong, Energetic, Funny, Wise, Free, Peaceful, Smart, Creative, Confident, Wise, Grateful, Easy, Healthy, Wealthy, Inspired, Excited

For the next day or two, think about how you want to feel and start a list:

Now, start acting the way you want to feel.

P.S. You can't get it wrong and it will be an ever-changing thing! Whew, right?!

WHAT'S THE STORY YOU'RE TELLING?

It's your story – Tell an epic one!

You get to choose your story. No matter what anyone says, you and only you can choose the story you tell yourself. You get to choose how you feel no matter what, and how you feel is what creates your own wonderful story.

What if you could make up a great story about you and who you would like to be and how you would like to live, and you started seeing evidence of it coming true in your life? That would be pretty awesome, right? Once you learn these powerful tools you will be able to visualize what you desire and attract those situations easily. How could that possibly happen you ask? If you know that everything is energy, and you really come to know that your thoughts, either positive or negative, attract to you like you are a magnet, you will see the proof right before your own eyes. Things and situations show up for you.

Appreciate everything

The highs, the lows, the ups, the downs are all worthy of your appreciation, even if it is hard to believe sometimes.

Start with making a list of all the things you do appreciate. From little things like; I love my favorite blanket, or the beautiful moon, to the big things; like an award for something you've accomplished, or a sweet new iPad. The sky's the limit on things to appreciate. They are everywhere, in every moment, if you notice and acknowledge them. And here's a bonus: You will attract more of those types of experiences because of your attention to them.

EXERCISE //
MY AWESOME LIFE

Here is a fun exercise or process for you to try. It really sets the stage for both your current and future success and happiness!

Grab a pen and paper and a timer set for 10 minutes.

Now smile, stretch, breathe, and align; this will be fun!

1. Pick any present or future, age or time for yourself: 25? 50? 100?, it doesn't matter.

2. Now, create a simple, short starter or opening sentence.

ex.: "As I walk along the beach I _____."

or; "I am so excited, because tonight I am _____.

or; "It is so fun to be living this life I've created. I just _____."

Just start anywhere, with anything, to get a story started.

3. Once you have your opening sentence, start your timer.

Don't hesitate, think ahead, or over-think as you create this future story of you.

Just write, non-stop for the full 10 minutes.

Even if what you are writing doesn't make sense or has grammatical errors, keep on telling the future story of you.

Make your story as big as you want!

This isn't an exercise to write the perfect story or to get it "right," this is to a process that will help your mind to flow and create ideas and thoughts as you write.

Just feel good in the process and see what shows up.

You might be surprised.

And if nothing comes of it, nothing lost and no worries. Try again sometime when you feel really aligned or light-hearted.

This isn't serious business friends; it is FUN and that is all that matters.

When you are done, throw the paper away or keep it if you wish.

If the story of you feels inspired or exciting and you want to keep it or continue writing it, then do so!

> **DREAM IT. BELIEVE IT. SEE IT. AND THE PATHWAYS WILL LIGHT UP FOR YOU, DIRECTING YOU, AS YOU MOVE WITH EASE AND FREEDOM THROUGH LIFE.**

YOU GET TO CHOOSE

What if I make a mistake in my choosing, or what I want doesn't show up?

You can't make a mistake and you can't get it wrong. Every situation that seems negative is really a powerful teacher showing you more clearly what you do want. And it is when you know what you don't want, that what you do want becomes clear. And being clear about what you do want is a superpower.

Magical thinking makes you a Master Manifester: What do you choose?

You get to choose the life you want to live. Sure, while you are young you may not have as many opportunities to actually choose, based on what others–parents, teachers, coaches, etc.–want or expect from you, but
you probably have more choices than you think.

You have far more power and control than you could ever imagine. You will come to understand this by giving it a try with small things.

EXERCISE // VISIONING

As always when doing the exercises, you want to be sure to get into a positive, aligned state first.

Write down something that you would like to be, do, or have.

Now take a few deep breaths and imagine that being your reality.

Notice how great it feels?

Even though that thing has not yet manifested, or happened, it feels awesome when you think about it doesn't it?

It is when you are in that good feeling place, aligned and easy, not worrying about how or when it will show up, that the energy that brings it all about is flowing and it feels like it is real, which in time brings it about.

Just enjoy that visioning and that feeling as much and as often as you can.

This exercise, as all the exercises in this book, are meant to be practiced again and again.

If you don't enjoy an exercise, don't do it.

You get to choose.

If you can't get to an aligned state, don't worry, try again later or just be patient with it.

You can't get it wrong!

THINGS ARE ALWAYS WORKING OUT FOR ME. -esther hicks

If you take nothing from this book, please consider at least this one saying. If you choose to believe this to be true, you will have a joyous adventure! Cj loves it so much, she made it into quote boards and gave them to her three oldest granddaughters (Lily included) so they would be able to read and live it every day.

SERIOUSLY... LIFE IS FUN!

Be easy about everything

Does this sound crazy to you? It's ok. Shifts in thinking take time and practice. Be patient with yourself and others and know that you are mastering the art of alignment. You can choose happy in each moment and when you do that, you live a happy life.

Get Happy Now!!!

AFTERWORD

Dear friends,

It really is all about love. It is loving yourself, loving those around you, and even loving those who seem unlovable. Just allow them to be who they are and send your good energy into the universe, for everyone. Love, play, work, dream and have fun doing it all!

Not everyone is ready for this information. In fact, some will say things like, "Oh that stuff is just a way of not facing reality, or sticking your head in the sand, or wishy, washy thinking," and that is perfectly ok. It is not up to you to teach it. They aren't going to understand it, but one thing is absolutely certain: it is a universal law and when you choose to look at everything in the best light, no matter what is going on, you will have powerful, attracting, positive energy flow, and that will create the happy ending you read about in fairy tales.

Just go about life, Happy Now, Happy Now, Happy Now, attracting all that you desire. You are a leader by your example. So, get out there, do your own Cakewalk, have fun, live your wildest dreams, and be easy about everything!

And remember—

"You can't get it wrong, and you never get it done" Abraham-Hicks

Seriously... Life is Fun!

With Joy, Fun, & Love,

Cj and Lily

REMEMBER TO SHARE

You're Invited to share! Share your stories with us! We may include them in our next book!

If you have a situation where you were able to use these Law of Attraction tools and practices to stay in alignment, continue to feel good, and have fun, please share your story with us! Who knows, your story may be featured in our next book! How fun would it be to see your story and know that it inspired or maybe helped someone else?! Cool, right?!

Simply start noticing more what is going on and how you are feeling. If there is something that bothers you or has been a problem for you in the past, pay attention to that and try shifting your thoughts, energy, and behavior to a more positive state of being. Then notice how positive things start occurring in your life. Also, notice how you affect the energy of those around you in a positive way. Notice all of it and write it down. We would love to hear from you about the positive shifts and outcomes you have.

Hey, Parents, we invite you as well to share stories or what changes you have seen in your teen/tween. We would love to hear from you as well! Submit your story via:

· **Website:** www.cakewalklife.com

· **Email us at:** contact@cakewalklife.com

Note: Even though the stories chosen will be uplifting and positive, we will only be using first names in book two, to protect all individuals, including us, as our audience mainly consists of those under 18 years of age. We will contact you if your story has been chosen.

We can't wait to hear from you!! Get out there and be your awesome, happy, aligned self!! You are changing the world!

GIVING BACK

We believe in sharing with others as one way to live a joy-filled and fun life.

That is why we have chosen to donate **$.50 from each book sold** to a charity that supports children.

We have chosen to support:
FEED MY STARVING CHILDREN https://www.fmsc.org/
Founded in 1987, Feed My Starving Children (FMSC) is a Christian non-profit that provides nutritionally complete meals specifically formulated for malnourished children.

RESOURCES AND RECOMMENDATIONS

Abraham Hicks. Of course our number 1 favorite resource, in case you may not have noticed, is Abraham Hicks. www.abraham-hicks.com. On their website, you will find their books and information about their events. You can find them on Facebook, Instagram, YouTube, and Twitter. They also have a daily quote they send via email that is a perfect way to stay on track.

The Hidden Messages in Water MASARU EMOTO, PG. 13

Tut – The Universe MIKE DOOLEY HTTP://WWW.TUT.COM/INSPIRATION/NFTU, PGS. 14 & 15

Steal like an Artist AUSTIN KLEON, PG. 21

tbh   THIS APP, "TO BE HONEST" IS "THE ONLY ANONYMOUS APP WITH POSITIVE VIBES" – ITUNES – APPLE

ABOUT CJ

Cj is a Certified Life Coach, "Joyful Living Coach" and has a passion for personal growth and development. She loves empowering others to live their best lives. She has always been interested in how and why we do the things we do and discovering how to change the patterns that do not assist or allow us to live amazing lives.

Cj has studied Abraham-Hicks Law of Attraction for more than 16 years, as well as the teachings of many other brilliant individuals.

She lives in Minnesota with her husband Jeremiah, who is a chiropractor and also a lover of learning, so overall mental and physical health and wellness is how they play in their daily lives.

– Oh, and so is having Fun!

ABOUT LiLY

Lily, 17, is a student at Westonka High School in Mound, Minnesota. She loves photography or anything else that involves being creative and plans to pursue her creative endeavors in college after graduation. She lives with her mom, Tina and dad, Shawn and sister Dalaney, as well as with their two boxers, Hazel and Zeus. Lily has always been a glass half-full kind of person, so when she started studying LOA it explained a lot. She has studied Abraham Hicks-Law of attraction for about five years now, where she learned how to look at life in a whole new positive way. She hopes this book will be a way for young people to understand, and relate LOA to their real life, so they can apply it to make life and situations lighter.

THANK YOU

From Cj:

First of all, I want to thank my dear first-born granddaughter and co-author, Lily. You amaze me with your ever-present sweetness, love, and kindness. You truly are a blessing not only to myself, and to our family, but to everyone you come in contact with. Your understanding of who you are, and positive energy, exudes from you, and has an impact on everyone you are around. I appreciate your dedication to this project. You wholeheartedly said yes, and never wavered in your desire to put this information out there to help others live a more aligned, fun, and happy life. You are also such a talented photographer, artist, and creative soul. You do beautiful work. I can't wait for book two!

I love you to the moon and back!

To my darling, insightful, inspiring, husband and love, Jeremiah, I can't imagine doing any of this without you. You inspire me daily and love me even when I don't feel loveable. Your support and guidance not only during this process, but in all that I do, is also unwavering. You have my love and appreciation every moment of every day. I know, for certain, that I am the luckiest person in the world! I Love You Always, and All Ways!

To my beautiful granddaughters Dalaney, and Kylee. Thank you from the bottom of my heart for your openness and generosity when we have conversations. You have helped this writing more than you know. You are both beautiful examples to others of how positive energy works, and you shine your light on those you interact with. And to Avery and Parker: you remind us to be childlike. You are all so loved and adored. I am so blessed to be your Yaya!

From Lily:

I want to Thank my grandma "Yaya" for introducing me to the powerful tool of Law of Attraction. She has always been a positive person who I look up to and I'm lucky to have been able to learn from her in the process of writing this book.

My whole family has been a big support in our process of writing the book. I want to thank my sister Laney for being a supportive sister and best friend. She makes me laugh the hardest and never fails to cheer me up! We act like dorks when we are together which makes for some entertaining times!

Lastly, I want to thank my awesome friends and my cousins, Kylee, Avery, Parker, & Charlie. for helping me out with the photos, and also for meeting up for brainstorming sessions. I appreciate your excitement and enthusiasm through this process!

FROM US

To our incredible friends and family who continually support and love us in all our endeavors. It is a long and lovely list. We hope you know you are loved and appreciated. To wonderful friends and family who shared stories with us and were our wonderful photography models! You are awesome!

To our "Book Doula", Kelly Pratt, of The So do it! Society. Thank you for helping us give birth to this project. We could not have done this without you. Your vision, creativity, and ability to connect on every level, made this a "Cakewalk". To our editor Sharon Payne, our design editor Heidi Miller of Heidi Miller Design, and Nancy Hendrickson of Wojack Hendrickson Design. You ladies seriously rock!! Thank you all for helping make this a reality!

OUR FAMILY

CAKEWALK UNIVERSITY

GRADUATE IN THE PRACTICE OF LAW OF ATTRACTION

CERTIFICATE OF AWESOMENESS

This certifies that

_____

YOUR NAME HERE

has successfully achieved alignment.
Love, Ease, Fun, and Joy are now available to you any time.

Congrats to you on this outstanding achievement!